Original title:
Soil Songs

Copyright © 2025 Creative Arts Management OÜ
All rights reserved.

Author: Milo Harrington
ISBN HARDBACK: 978-1-80581-934-9
ISBN PAPERBACK: 978-1-80581-461-0
ISBN EBOOK: 978-1-80581-934-9

The Breath of Flora

In the garden where weeds go wild,
Plants giggle and sway, like a child.
Worms roll over in the rich, dark bed,
Tickling the roots of a sleepy red.

Murmurs of Essence

The daisies dance in a sunny parade,
While ants cha-cha, their plans well laid.
The clouds above are a fluffy crew,
Dropping raindrops like candy, just for a view.

Layers of Existence

Paths of dirt are like life's great book,
Each inch tells a tale if you take a look.
Rabbits hold a tea party by the tree,
While mushrooms plot their next great spree.

The First Note of Spring

A tiny bud peeks with a cheeky grin,
Saying, 'Hey world, let the fun begin!'
The bees wear hats, buzzing with flair,
As flowers throw a fragrant fair.

Growing in the Silence

In the garden where whispers play,
The daisies giggle, come what may.
A worm does the cha-cha under the dirt,
While ants parade in their tiny shirt.

The carrots debate whether to sprout,
As snails grumble softly, 'What's that about?'
Clouds loom overhead, their jokes sublime,
While weeds practice stand-up, one line at a time.

A Dance of Decay

Leaves twirl down in a jazzy fall,
While mushrooms mount their fungal ball.
Old apples rotting, sharing a grin,
Invite the critters to come and spin.

An earthworm sighs, it's his big break,
As compost joins in, for goodness' sake!
A dance of decay, a merry shindig,
Every squishy bit twirls with a wig.

Harmonizing the Earth's Palette

Roses blush, while daisies hum,
The marigolds join in — oh, what fun!
Crickets strum on their grassy lute,
While radishes jiggle in root-toot-toot.

A rainbow spills over the plot,
As veggies throw confetti — oh, they're hot!
Tomatoes roll out in their shiny red,
In the garden concert, nothing's dead!

The Understory Whisper

The ferns are gossiping under the shade,
About squirrels and their nutty crusade.
A soft breeze chuckles, rustling the leaves,
While mushrooms listen, donning their sleeves.

Jitterbugs waltz on the forest floor,
While roots murmur secrets, evermore.
With each silly shuffle, the understory grins,
In this funny realm, everyone wins!

The Dance of the Dirt

In the garden, worms do twirl,
They wiggle, they jive, give the soil a whirl.
Rocks are nodding, pebbles do sway,
Nature's party, come join the play.

Ants in tuxedos march like a crew,
Throwing a picnic, just for you.
Beetles tap dance on sticks for a tune,
While the sun sneezes and tickles the moon.

Grooves in the Gravel

Gravel grins beneath my feet,
Creating rhythms, oh so sweet!
Each stone a DJ, spinning right,
Bumping and grinding, oh what a sight!

Rabbits jump in a line, so spry,
As the rocks chuckle, they can't deny.
Crickets chirp with jazzy flair,
In this groove, we haven't a care.

Rhapsody of the Ruins

Old bricks whisper tales from the past,
Remnants of laughter, shadows cast.
Lizards perform, scaling the walls,
While ivy wraps like a curtain that falls.

Mice in capes play thief in the night,
Stealing crumbs, what a delightful sight!
The ruins chuckle as time slips away,
In a grand concert, they dance and sway.

Songs of the Seedlings

Tiny sprouts break through the ground,
Singing sweet nothings, what a sound!
Their leaves are swaying, breezy and bold,
Telling tales of sunshine, stories of old.

A dandelion with dreams so high,
Wants a ride on the back of the sky.
These merry seedlings, with smiles so wide,
Remind us that laughter cannot hide.

The Pulse of the Panorama

The worms are dancing, oh so bold,
With tiny boots on amber gold.
They twirl around, a lively crew,
In mud they prance, not minding you.

The daisies giggle with delight,
As earthworms spin beneath the light.
A spectacle, such joy I see,
A merry farce, from A to Z.

Nature's Secret Symphony

The crickets chirp a cheeky tune,
While moles keep time beneath the moon.
The ants march on, their tiny feet,
Creating grooves, oh what a feat!

A squirrel laughs from up the tree,
He drops a nut, now what a spree!
The forest buzzes with such glee,
A concert grand, for you and me!

The Music of Decomposition

Fallen leaves rustle, they have a say,
In the compost bin, they dance and play.
Banana peels hum a lively jig,
As critters join, they all come big.

The fungi strum on broken twigs,
While beetles waltz, they wiggle and dig.
Garbage a symphony, life's embrace,
In every nook, a merry place!

Ancestral Echoes in the Loam

Grandpa's roots tell tales so wise,
Of beetles buzzing and squishy pies.
He chuckles deep as earthworms swirl,
In tales of dirt where treasures unfurl.

With each soft whisper, seeds do dream,
Of sprouting high, a veggie team.
The past sings funny in the ground,
Where laughter blooms, and life is found.

Seeds of Harmony

In the garden, gnomes do dance,
With veggies growing, they take a chance.
Radishes giggle, carrots play,
Under sunbeams, they shout hooray!

The beans are jumping, so spry and bold,
Telling tales of the young and old.
Peas in a pod make a funny sound,
As they bounce around the fertile ground.

Unfolding Echoes

Worms are philosophers in a wriggly way,
Musing on life's dirt as they sway.
Beneath the clouds, they stretch and twist,
Muttering secrets that none can resist.

The seedlings stand in a crooked line,
Each one waiting for a sign.
They tease the beetles with a wiggly jive,
In their quirky world, they feel alive.

Buzzing Beneath the Surface

Beneath the ground, a party brews,
Ants bust moves in their funky shoes.
Bees mix honey with giggles and cheers,
While root systems dance without any fears.

The fungi are chefs in a dirt-based show,
Cooking up flavors only worms know.
Everyone's laughing while sipping some dew,
In this merry land of the hidden crew.

Musical Morsels of Life

The radish plays the tambourine,
While potatoes trot in a sprightly scene.
Zucchinis strum on grass blades high,
As mushrooms hum tunes that touch the sky.

With laughter sprouting from each little root,
They throw a ball with a fresh, sweet fruit.
Moments of joy sprout all around,
In this whimsical world underground!

A Tidal Wave of Earthly Voices

In the garden, worms are prancing,
Dancing roots are quite enhancing.
The carrots giggle, peas take flight,
While radishes wear crowns at night.

The beetroot blushes, joking free,
Says, "Don't my stalks look good on me?"
While onions chuckle, shedding tears,
As leafy greens toast to their years.

A dandelion whispers about its fame,
"I'm the pop star in this leafy game!"
Sunflowers laugh, heads held so high,
Content to tickle the blue sky.

In this earthy, silly parade,
Life below the surface is well-played.
With every seed, a story told,
In this tapestry, bright and bold.

Sweet Refrains of the Past

In the garden where the lettuce grows,
A cabbage whispered all its woes.
Carrots giggled under their breath,
Dirt in the air, but no sign of death.

Turnips danced with a radish flair,
While peas blew bubbles floating in air.
Tomatoes wore hats, oh what a sight,
Merriment buzzing from morning till night.

Remnants of Respiration

Earthworms wiggled, doing the twist,
Each squirm a part of nature's list.
Beneath the ground, they plot and scheme,
Life in the dirt, like a wild dream.

A beetle lugged a crumb with pride,
While ants held a dance on the side.
With giggles and winks, they swayed to the beat,
Nature's odd party, where dirt folks meet.

Strains of Starlit Soil

The moonlight whispered to the green beans,
Dreaming of places where no one has seen.
Cucumbers chuckled, their laughter a tune,
Under the gaze of a friendly moon.

Radishes grinned in their leafy beds,
While a turnip told tales that spun in their heads.
With each little poke of a spade from afar,
They all joined together, the soil's own stars.

The Sanctuary Beneath

Critters in the dirt, what a wild bunch,
Throwing a shindig with roots for lunch.
A potato served chips, oh what a treat,
While mushrooms swayed to the underground beat.

Beneath the vines, silly secrets are kept,
Where the funniest gophers have often wept.
In their cozy lair, so snug and so spry,
A laugh in the earth, twinkling up to the sky.

Melodic Tides of the Abode

The worms in the dirt play a tune,
They wiggle and squirm, dancing all afternoon.
Under the rays of the bright sun's glow,
They plot their mischief, putting on a show.

Grass blades whisper to the bees up high,
They gossip and giggle, oh me, oh my!
The daisies start clapping, the violets sway,
As ants hold a parade, on this fine day.

Crickets bring rhythm, frogs join the beat,
The earth really knows how to party and eat.
With roots on the ground and leaves in the air,
The merry ensemble can't help but share!

So sing with the critters in this lush grove,
Join in their laughter, no need to be shy.
For nature's a stage where the silly abide,
Unfolding their songs like a jolly tide.

Cadence of the Canopy

In the treetops, a squirrel sings loud,
He mimics the wind, puts on quite a crowd.
With acorns and nuts, he jigs and jives,
While the branches sway, oh how he thrives!

The leaves wear their shimmies like party hats,
While the owls hoot tunes, getting all the spats.
Bamboo steals the spotlight, dancing with glee,
As vines twist and twirl like a wild jubilee.

Funky fungi pop up, they join in too,
With colors so bright, they steal the view.
As shadows play games, hide and seek in the sun,
Laughter erupts, oh what comedic fun!

In this lively realm, no reason to pout,
Nature's the stage, there's not a doubt.
So bring out your giggles, let the joy flow,
And dance with the trees, let that spirit grow.

Beneath the Boughs

A snail in a shell sings a slow ballad,
While mushrooms crack jokes, oh what a salad!
The shadows spread laughter like daisies in bloom,
Beneath the green curtain, there's never a gloom.

The rabbits tap feet on the soft, grassy floor,
As crickets all cheer with a symphonic roar.
The ladybugs gossip about who wore what,
While caterpillars groove, giving it a shot.

Then comes a hedgehog, his dance is quite quirky,
With wiggly moves, he's never too jerky.
The ants form a line, it's a neat little train,
In this fun little corner, there's only gain!

So cuddle with laughter as the sun slips away,
Amongst all the chirping, let your cares sway.
For under the boughs, the joy is around,
A circus of nature where fun's always found.

The Heartbeat of the Hollow

There's a frog on a lily, croaking a beat,
As fireflies twinkle like stars in the heat.
The pond joins a chorus, so lively and spry,
Making music together, oh me, oh my!

The cattails sway gently, they hum along,
To the rhythm of crickets, a whimsical song.
With raccoons in tuxes, they steal the scene,
In this hollow of laughter, where all is serene.

The mushrooms start to tango, they pair up for fun,
While beetles do the hustle, under the sun.
Each ripple and giggle creates a delight,
A jovial spotlight shines through the night.

So join in the revelry, don't be so shy,
In this merry hollow, let your spirits fly.
With creatures a-chatter, the jokes on the air,
Together we celebrate, laughter to share!

Echoes from the Underworld

A worm wiggled with glee, oh what a sight,
He found a carrot and said, "This feels just right!"
The ants threw a party, in circles they danced,
While beetles played music, all night they pranced.

The fungi wore hats and they sang with flair,
They laughed as the raindrops fell down like hair.
A snail on a trumpet, so slow yet so grand,
Gave concerts each evening to all in the land.

The moles played charades, a burrowing game,
While roots whispered secrets, playing it tame.
Each creature agreed that a ruckus was fun,
Beneath all that dirt, there's a wild, quirky run.

So if you dig deep, where the shadows run bright,
You'll find hidden gems in the dark and the light.
With echoes of laughter beneath your two feet,
Remember, the underworld also knows sweet!

Melodies of the Untamed Ground

There's a ticklish daisy, oh what a tease,
It laughs at the breeze, with whimsical ease.
The grasses are giggling, they sway side to side,
As odd little creatures go out for a ride.

The crickets are busy, they tap dance in pairs,
With songbirds that chirp like they haven't a care.
A toad croaks the bass, what a jazzy affair,
While ladybugs twirl without any despair.

The sunshine's a spotlight, for all to see,
As nature's own orchestra plays joyfully.
A shovel's a baton, directing all sound,
In this lively concert from deep underground.

So come join the fun, and bring all your cheer,
In this jolly symphony, there's nothing to fear.
For melodies rise, from what's hidden and found,
In the whimsical tunes of the untamed ground.

Lullabies of Loam

As the moonlight shines down on the patchy old yard,
The roots hum a lullaby with the sweetest regard.
The sleepy small critters, all cuddled in beds,
Nestle close to each other, resting their heads.

The stones tell a tale of a journey they made,
From mountains to valleys, to crags they have played.
With whispers of breezes, they sigh just so sweet,
In this cozy embrace at nature's heartbeat.

The wildflowers drowse, their petals so bright,
As crickets sing softly, bidding day goodbye.
Each twinkling star up, a wink from above,
Reminds us of magic and comforting love.

So drift off, dear dreamers, to that hidden bliss,
Where loam rocks the cradle, and all worry's amiss.
In the gentle embrace of this nighttime show,
Rest your head and let laughter and sweet dreams overflow.

Notes of Nature's Canvas

With a splash of the mud, what a painting we make,
The worms are the brushes, oh what a mistake!
A dandelion laughs as it gets in the mix,
"Watch out for the splatter!" it shouts with a flick.

Each raindrop's a note in the symphonic show,
Where bees do the ballet, oh what a flow!
A butterfly flutters, adding colors so bright,
While shadows of plants dance in soft morning light.

The roots write a story, in cryptic old scripts,
As lizards take selfies, with stylish little flips.
A swing on a leaf, oh the fun never ends,
In a gallery of laughter where all nature blends.

So take out your canvas and let nature play,
Join the giggling critters, don't shy away.
For in every deep corner, there's laughter to find,
In notes of this canvas, we're all intertwined!

Silent Hymns of the Ground

Down below where the critters dance,
Earthworms wiggle, lost in trance.
Grubby roots play their funky beat,
While ants march on with wiggly feet.

A mole in his cap, scepter in hand,
Declares himself ruler of this land.
The grass giggles underfoot,
As daisies strut in fancy boots.

Rocks hum a tune of ages past,
In this realm where laughter lasts.
Each pebble's joke, a crack so dry,
Makes the boulders laugh and sigh.

So take a seat on this merry mound,
Join the chuckles of the ground.
For in this patch of earthy spree,
Life's a joke, just wait and see!

The Spirit of the Silt

In a puddle sits a muddy sprite,
Flipping tadpoles with pure delight.
He calls out jokes, splashes abound,
Laughter echoes all around.

With a splash and a giggle, the water bugs spin,
Who knew mud could make such a din?
Grass blades shrug their leafy heads,
As daisies roll over, cracking up instead.

A snail with a top hat, oh what a sight,
Slips on a gnat in his high-speed flight.
"Is this a race? I'm fitting to win!"
He shouts with glee, as he tumbles in.

So raise a cup of dandelion tea,
To those mud puddles, wild and free.
Let's toast to giggles in silt's embrace,
A party of dirt in this happy place!

Whispers from the Wildflower Patch

Petals gossip in whispers low,
Telling tales of bees in tow.
"Did you see that? The insect fell!
He thought he could dance — oh what a swell!"

Butterflies flutter, sharing a giggle,
As ladybugs play tag and wiggle.
"Catch me if you can!" one shouts with glee,
But all agree they dance like me.

A sleepy bloom dreams of cake and cream,
While daisies plot a fashion scheme.
"Let's wear hats made of dew drops bright!
Garden chic is our style tonight!"

So next time you plop in a meadow vast,
Listen close, let the flowers cast.
Their joyful banter, a sweet delight,
Will tickle your heart and feel just right!

Odes to the Organic

In the compost pile, a choir sings,
With worms and beetles showcasing rings.
"Who knew scraps could make such a show?
With laughter and flocks, let's make it glow!"

Carrots gossip in rows so neat,
"Watch out for that sneaky veggie cheat!"
With leafy hats, they play their parts,
Growing wise with earthy arts.

The potatoes joke, 'We're on a roll!'
While onions cry, "It's all our goal!"
They stir a pot full of playful spice,
Adding joy to every slice.

So let us toast to nature's fun,
An organic party for everyone!
With belly laughs, plants can thrive,
In this wild and silly life!

Chants of the Buried

In the dark, a worm does twirl,
Dancing round with a leafy girl.
They sing of grub and slugs so sly,
Making dirt clods laugh and sigh.

A beetle struts with a shiny grin,
Proclaiming every bug's a win.
While roots below play peek-a-boo,
In their kingdom, they brew a stew.

Ants march in a quirky line,
Carrying crumbs, oh what a dine!
They gossip low in a silly spree,
Worms are clumsy, can't you see?

But when it rains, the party's wild,
Mushrooms pop up, nature's child.
With a splash and a squish, they cheer aloud,
In their underground, they're really proud.

Rooted Reverie

Beneath the ground, a tale unfolds,
Where secrets hide, and mischief molds.
A radish dreams of being a star,
But ends up just a salad jar.

The carrots gossip in vibrant hues,
While peas debate the latest news.
With roots entwined, they share a laugh,
"Who's the funniest? Oh, it's the gaff!"

Potatoes dress in muddy suits,
Strutting 'round like fancy brutes.
They boast of how they're often fried,
While in the dirt, they've often lied.

Oh, the laughter in their green delight,
As tiny sprouts reach for the light.
In the ground's embrace, they find their joy,
Each tale retold, like a playful ploy.

The Language of Layers

Down below, in the earth's wide hall,
The tales are told, they enthrall.
A mole hums tunes in a shaky tone,
While pebbles sit, feeling overgrown.

Worms chat in whispers, quick and sly,
Joking about the time they flew high.
"Dig deeper, mate!" they slyly sing,
As bugs tap dance to the drumming spring.

With each layer, there's giggly cheer,
The family of fungi joins near.
With hats of moss, and coats of grime,
They cheer for all in perfect rhyme.

The gophers hold a burrowed fest,
With snacks of soil, they are the best.
All piled together, a merry crew,
In the earth's embrace, all feels brand new.

Riffs of the Rainfall

Pitter-patter, raindrops fall,
Dancing critters heed the call.
Worms glide in a slippery glide,
While puddles become the joyride.

Amidst the dappled drops, they slip,
Ants take cover in a raindrop dip.
"There's a pool party for all we say!"
As muddy boots jump in the fray.

The snails lead line, all shiny and slick,
While mushrooms pop some fancy tricks.
"I'm the umbrella, oh can't you see?"
But underneath, they're just plain glee!

As nature hums its playful tune,
With laughter shared beneath the moon.
Each drip and drop a merry sound,
In the joy of earth, laughter abound.

Tapestry of Life Below

In the garden where worms reside,
They're plotting an underground slide.
With roots as their funky attire,
They dance in the dirt like they're wired.

Ants hold a parade on a leaf,
In tiny hats, they find their belief.
They march to the beat of a hidden drum,
While the grubs laugh and wiggle their bum.

A snail slips in with style so grand,
Painting the town with a sticky hand.
While beetles boast of their shiny shells,
Trading tales of their muddy dwells.

In this land where the critters sway,
Life's a party in the clay!
From the tiniest root to the tallest tree,
All of them dance—come join the spree!

Cadence of the Clay

The worms in their homes go 'squiggle-squirm',
As they plan out their evening term.
While fungi throw a fuzzy bash,
And tell the jokes that make you crash.

A mole digs a tunnel — what a delight!
He shouts, "I can hide—out of sight!"
With a top hat made of mud so neat,
He claims he's the king of this funky beat.

Caterpillars wiggle on leafy chairs,
Debating who styles their hair with flares.
In such soil debate, they're quite clever,
Laughter that stretches on forever.

So in the clay, let the humors flow,
With each little critter putting on a show.
A joyful jive beneath our toes,
In the dance party where nature glows!

Harmonies in the Humus

Underneath the leafy sheets,
Tiny critters tap their feet.
A cricket sings a dainty tune,
While mice chuckle at the moon.

The beetles, in their royal ball,
Strut and brag, they're ten feet tall.
While tiny ants bring lunch to share,
As they dash around without a care.

A ladybug joins with a polka flair,
Whirling 'round like she's lost her air.
And all the plants sway left and right,
Enjoying this wild, whimsical sight.

With laughter echoing through the din,
Nature's concert is about to begin.
In the rich passages beneath our feet,
A funny fest that can't be beat!

The Knots of Nature

Tangled roots twist in a comical way,
They're tying their shoes for a muddy play.
While over the top, the branches sway,
As squirrels laugh, "We're here all day!"

A raccoon attempts to steal a snack,
As worms plot a counterattack.
"Oh no," says the snail, "Not again!"
While laughter erupts from a nearby fen.

The daisies gossip about their blooms,
Saying, "Look at us, we're the best of tombs!"
With every giggle in the ground's embrace,
Nature's humor shines in every space.

So let's all chuckle at the mess we make,
In the knots of nature where friendships wake.
Together we frolic in this fertile bed,
With smiles and giggles, let's all be fed!

Earth's Whispered Melodies

In the garden, worms do dance,
Making moves that take a chance.
With tiny hats and coats so bright,
They wiggle left, they wiggle right.

Poking noses out to play,
They giggle softly, come what may.
With munching bugs as their sweet prey,
They dream of dirt in a sassy way.

The daisies hum a cheerful tune,
Beneath the sun and laughing moon.
As ants parade with tiny drums,
The earth replies with joyful hums.

Dandelions join in the song,
Singing loud, they can't go wrong.
In this chorus, all are friends,
Where laughter blooms and never ends.

Beneath the Surface

Beneath the ground, the critters scheme,
Building tunnels, what a dream!
With tiny shovels made of leaf,
They dig away, beyond belief.

A mole in shades prepares to dig,
While others dance a wormy jig.
An earthworm stretches, feeling proud,
To be the star of this big crowd.

The beetles roll their shiny balls,
While crickets chirp their silly calls.
With every wiggle and each dive,
They throw a fun, underground jive.

If you can hear them laugh and play,
You'd join their antics any day.
Beneath the surface, let it be,
A party waits entirely free!

Harmonies of the Humus

In every layer, secrets dwell,
A symphony that weaves so well.
With every leaf and twinkling beetle,
They compose a tune, oh so sweetly subtle.

The grubs are drummers, soft and low,
While ants keep time with a steady flow.
A mushroom sings with spores in flight,
In this bizarre, delightful plight.

The roots are strumming, bending down,
Providing melodies all around.
While meadow flowers giggle bright,
Their gentle songs ease day to night.

In harmony where critters roam,
The rich dark earth feels just like home.
A concert hall beneath our feet,
With melodies so fresh and sweet.

The Roots' Reverie

In tangled dance, the roots entwine,
Creating chaos, oh so fine.
They giggle softly in the night,
Planning mischief with delight.

A vine, a sprout, all in a race,
Tangle up, create a space.
With leafy hats and fluttering dreams,
They swap their tales in joyful themes.

The daisies peek, their heads held high,
As roots recite their tales nearby.
"A carrot once thought it was a star,
But grew too short, now here we are!"

In this reverie of green and brown,
The roots have fun while wearing crowns.
A party nestled deep below,
Where silly plants have room to grow.

The Rhythm of Renewal

In the garden, we do dance,
Earthworms wiggling, take a chance.
With a shovel and some cheer,
Digging deep, we have no fear.

Seeds are popping, what a sight,
Sprouting leaves, oh what a night!
Funny how the plants all grin,
Each one hoping for a win.

Rain drops tap in perfect time,
A rhythm sweet as nursery rhyme.
Daffodils in funny hats,
Strutting 'round like fancy cats.

Rabbits hop in playful leaps,
Chasing shadows while the peep.
Nature laughs, with vibrant tone,
The earth's a stage, we're not alone.

Patches of Silence

In patches where the daisies bloom,
A quiet space to fend off gloom.
Grass blades whisper, soft and low,
Tickling toes as breezes blow.

Squirrels plotting in the trees,
Dropping acorns, just for tease.
In a moment, silence reigns,
Then a giggle, life, it gains.

Bees are buzzing in a flight,
Joking 'round till fall of night.
Nature's laughter fills the air,
Honey-sweet, without a care.

Watch the flowers tell their jokes,
Beneath the sun, it's not a hoax.
Together, we all share a space,
In this quiet, funny place.

A Chorus of Worms

Worms unite in wriggly song,
In the mud, where they belong.
With a slither, what a sight,
They're the stars of the night.

Singing tunes of soft decay,
Making compost, hip-hip-hooray!
Little critters of the ground,
Funny rhythms all around.

Their voices hum a squishy beat,
As they travel, oh so neat.
Turning scraps to treasure bright,
Worms bringing joy, what a delight!

If you listen, truly hear,
Their laughter's music, bold and clear.
A choir in a loamy shawl,
Worms together, having a ball.

The Mournful Earth

Oh, the earth, it wears a frown,
Listening to the wind's sad sound.
Cracks and crevices, full of sighs,
Nature weeps, but that's no surprise.

Puddles form like teardrop pools,
Reflecting skies like solemn jewels.
Yet a worm gives a cheeky grin,
Telling tales where fun begins.

While the trees sway, hearts profess,
Nature's humor in the mess.
A fallen leaf, a twist of fate,
Cracks a smile on a gloomy slate.

So, laugh along when skies are gray,
The mournful earth can play today.
In every giggle, every sound,
Joy can flourish from the ground.

Voices from the Earth's Embrace

Wiggly worms sing in the dirt,
With a squiggly line and a happy flirt.
They dance in circles, oh what a sight,
Competing for space 'neath the moonlight.

The ants hold parties, with crumbs as snacks,
Jiving and thriving on all the green tracks.
With tiny top hats and a fancy bow,
They boogie down low where no one can go.

The rocks play poker, all tough and stony,
Betting their chips, feeling quite phony.
While roots gossip softly, sharing the scoop,
Launching wild tales of the underground troupe.

A rabbit hops by, with a curious ear,
Listening in on their gossip and cheer.
With laughter that tickles, the laughter that rolls,
Life underfoot has its own funny goals.

The Echo Chamber of Roots

Deep in the earth, where the giggles reside,
Roots tell tall tales of their sneaky glide.
They whisper to each other like kids at a play,
Trading sweet secrets in a silly way.

The mushrooms act posh, wearing hats made of dirt,
While daisies throw snickers at their fashion alert.
"With a sprinkle of rain and a pinch of regret,"
They strut down the path, without any fret.

Rocks roll their eyes, with a clatter and click,
While grass blades join chorus, each choosing a trick.
They tickle each other, with sunbeams and glee,
Together they laugh, oh what's left to see?

A playful debate on who's tallest of all,
With the burly oak tree making quite the call.
In the echo chamber where whimsy takes root,
Nature's loud laughter is simply a hoot!

Footsteps of Fertility

Bouncing potatoes with a grin,
Roll down the hill, oh let the fun begin!
With every sprout bursting loud in delight,
The garden's a dance floor, a curious sight.

The carrots wear shades, trying to be hip,
While beets try to spin, taking a trip.
"Look at us grow, we're the life of the feast!"
Shouts the proud radish, "To veggies, we toast this!"

Ladybugs laugh, on a leaf they reside,
Scribbling their memoirs, from side to side.
With stories so grand of all they have seen,
Underneath shadows where the grass blades O'Green.

Tiny seeds giggle, plotting their rise,
With promises of blooms that can light up the skies.
In footsteps of fertility, let laughter take flight,
With nature's own chorus, the joyful invite.

Serenade of the Subterranean

In the darkness below, where the funny folks hum,
The moles tap their toes to a merry old drum.
With chatter and cheers, they echo the sound,
Underground melodies, joyous and round.

The toads croak in chorus, while crickets provide,
A rhythm of life that they cannot abide.
"High five the dirt clod!" one toad croons loud,
Celebrating their party, feeling so proud.

The roots hum along, in their tangled ballet,
Twisting and turning in a whimsical way.
With laughter as fertile as the ground that they tread,
They raise up a tune, no one left unread.

From the tiniest bugs to the hugest of mounds,
They join in a jig that reverberates sounds.
In the serenade deep where the light is so rare,
The chorus of laughter floats up in the air.

The Ground's Gentle Murmur

The earth chuckles softly by the tree,
Whispers of dreams in the roots, you see.
Worms throw a party, oh what a sight!
Dancing in dirt till the morning light.

Ants in their suits march with such flair,
Collecting the crumbs, oh, they love to share.
While mushrooms giggle, sprouting so proud,
Tickled by raindrops—nature's loud crowd.

Grass blades gossip under the sun,
Teasing each other, oh, what fun!
With each gentle breeze, they sway and lean,
A comedy show in shades of green.

Beneath our feet, the jokes do abound,
Nature's stand-up—hilarity found!
So next time you tread on this merry ground,
Listen close, laughter's echo is profound.

Verses of the Verdant

A sunflower winked with a smile so wide,
While snails on their shells took a very slow ride.
The daisies debated on who was the best,
In the contest of pretty, they never do rest.

The clouds giggled down, with a sprinkle or two,
Tickling the petals, oh, how they flew!
A thistle in tights, prancing with glee,
Declared itself queen of the garden party.

Bees buzzed their tunes on sweet honey air,
While frogs croaked along as if they were rare.
A party of veggies joined in the fun,
Cabbage conga lines under the sun!

Laughter and color in every direction,
Nature's own circus, a true perfection.
So come join the chorus, pick up your feet,
In the verses of verdant, life's truly a treat.

The Symphony Beneath Our Feet

Listen closely, there's music here,
Frogs in the chorus, singing with cheer.
Crickets are drumming, with sticks made of grass,
While ants tap dance—oh, they sashay past!

A cheerful old mole plays a grand bassoon,
As beetles and bugs join the afternoon.
Peeking from puddles, the splashes compose,
Nature's sweet symphony, everyone knows.

A whirlwind of laughter, the leaves spin around,
As squirrels join in with their chirpy sound.
The flowers all hum with a lively refrain,
A delightful duet, joy in each grain!

When night falls down, the stars join the mix,
Fireflies flash tunes; they've got all the tricks.
In the whispers below, beneath soft moonlight,
The symphony thrives, oh what a delight!

Bards of the Barren

In the barren fields, the creatures convene,
Weird little bards, with stories unseen.
Cactus strumming tunes on a prickly guitar,
Echoes of laughter from afar.

A lizard in shades dons a sly little grin,
Reciting tall tales of adventures within.
While tumbleweeds roll, crafting their rhymes,
Sand whispers secrets through endless times.

The crows are the critics; they hop and they caw,
Judging the stories and having a draw.
With every tall tale, a chuckle they lend,
Bards of the barren, where laughter won't end.

So if you wander where the dry winds blow,
Stop for a moment, join the show.
For in every desolate patch you may find,
The humor of nature, refreshingly unconfined.

Chords of the Compost

In the compost heap, critters play,
Worms do dances, hip-hip-hooray!
Banana peels sing, apples hum,
Nutrient notes, a fruity strum.

Fungi strut, they know the groove,
Breaking down scraps, they find their move.
Dirt has rhythm, we laugh and cheer,
Nature's band is always near.

Twirling leaves in the autumn breeze,
Giggle with roots, as they tease.
In this muck, there's joy to find,
Nature's jester, one of a kind.

Sprouting plants join the merry show,
With each sprout, the laughter grows.
Dance of life in a funny sprawl,
Compost beats, let's have a ball!

The Beneath's Lyric

Down below where the earthworms dwell,
They sing of stories, oh, who can tell?
Roly-poly bugs cha-cha all day,
Moles dig deep, they sway and play.

Funky roots are kicking it back,
Dancing with rocks, keeping on track.
A beetle jiggles, with ant on guitar,
In the roots' band, they are the stars.

Nutrients jive, while rainworms prance,
Plant pals join in, oh what a dance!
Under our feet, the rhythm's strong,
In the dark, they sing their song.

So next time you walk, tap your feet,
Feel those beats, oh what a treat!
The beneath is alive, not shy at all,
In this raucous dance, we've got a ball!

Verdant Voices

Grassy patches crack jokes at dawn,
While daisies debate, 'Should we yawn?'
Clover giggles, sharing a cheer,
Whispering secrets for all to hear.

Thistles tell tales of mighty knights,
Fighting off weeds with all their might.
Buttercup chuckles, 'You won't believe,
Yesterday, I made a fox reprieve!'

The trees hum deep, their leaves clap loud,
While lilies prance, all charming and proud.
In the meadow, laughter does blend,
With every rustle, the jokes extend.

Nature's choir is quirky and sweet,
With funny verses, oh, what a treat!
Among the greens, joy does arise,
In verdant voices, laughter flies!

Whispers of the Wind and Earth

The breeze tickles leaves, a playful poke,
While earthworms giggle, sharing a joke.
"Look at that cloud, it's shaped like a cat!"
The daisies snicker, "Imagine that!"

Under the ground, a ruckus ensues,
Ants plot a party, with snacks to choose.
Caterpillars dance, wiggling bright,
Beneath the moon, in the cool of night.

Nature's antics create a play,
Where bugs and blooms all laugh away.
The harmony swells, as beetles swoon,
In whispers of joy, beneath the moon.

So take a stroll on this merry Earth,
Join in the laughter; oh, what a worth!
In whispers of life, both funny and grand,
Let's celebrate the joy at hand!

Beneath the Green Canopy

Underneath the leafy spreads,
Worms are wiggling in their beds.
Rabbits dance with quite a flair,
Squirrels giggle, do not care.

With the roots in all their glee,
Tell the bugs, come laugh with me!
Frogs in chorus, croak and croon,
Nature's night an offbeat tune.

Grasshoppers tweak the high notes right,
While ants march on, a silly sight.
In this merry, earthy place,
Every plant wears a smiling face.

So lift your head, breathe in the jest,
In this green space, we are blessed.
The canopy sounds, wild and free,
Funny whispers, just you and me.

The Earth's Lullaby

In the dark, the critters yawn,
Crickets chirp, the dusk is drawn.
Above the roots, the stars play tricks,
While moles work on their magic flicks.

With a blanket made of leaves,
The beetle hums as the wind weaves.
Dreams of worms in their tiny lairs,
As the earth chuckles, no one cares.

The sleepy plants begin to sway,
Rustling tales of a light-hearted day.
Each blade of grass hums softly, too,
Tickling toes as a night breeze blew.

Hushed, the world, it twists and turns,
With every giggle, the soil yearns.
In this lull, let the laughter rise,
For even nature shares its sighs.

Vibrations in the Dirt

Beneath our feet, the party starts,
Microbes dance with tiny hearts.
In the mud, they kick and slide,
Throwing smiles far and wide.

Bees play drums, buzz-buzz, they flee,
Making melodies, wild and free.
Grass roots twist in rhythmic time,
Tapping out a funky rhyme.

Earthworms wiggle, pulling tight,
Sharing jokes beneath the light.
Plants green-laugh, it's quite absurd,
In the dirt, they're never blurred.

With this vibe, let's sing along,
To the beat of nature's song.
In this soil, life takes a turn,
And the world smiles, it's our turn.

Songs of the Hidden Seed

In a pocket of the earth,
Lies a secret, a seed of mirth.
Snuggled down, it starts to dream,
Of jumping high, like a funny beam.

Nuts and fruits, they share their cheer,
The bushes grinning from ear to ear.
In this game, all roots compete,
For the silliest, hidden beat.

As the sprout shows its small green face,
It wiggles about, finds its space.
Shouting out to the sunlit morn,
Here comes the giggle of a corn!

Listen close to those whispers shy,
From the depths where the laughter lies.
Every seed has a tale to weave,
And in its joy, the world believes.

Secrets of the Subterranean

Worms are dancing in their tuxes,
Throwing parties with all the muck.
Rabbits join the underground rave,
Chasing shadows they misbehave.

Beneath the ground, a secret club,
Where moles and gophers share their grub.
The beetles hum, the ants all cheer,
While roots do the conga, oh dear!

Wiggly friends in a muddy throng,
Their shenanigans go on for long.
When you plant, just know they're near,
Throwing a bash; it's quite the cheer!

So if you dig, don't take it wrong,
Just join the fun, and sing a song.
With laughter mixed in earthy beats,
The ground is more than where life eats.

Rhythms of the Rain-soaked Earth

Puddles splash, and raindrops sway,
As frogs start croaking, hip-hip-hooray!
The worms do wiggle, tap their toes,
As thunder claps and mischief grows.

The grasses dance in swaying lines,
While crickets chirp in funny rhymes.
Each raindrop brings a jaunty beat,
As soil waltzes beneath our feet.

Slugs slide in their slimy shoes,
Declaring war on morning dews.
The roots do groove, each dance step spry,
As puddles catch the cloud-painted sky.

So next time rain's on your parade,
Listen close to the fun that's made.
For nature's party, rich and keen,
Is host to more than we have seen.

The Canvas of Nutrients

Colorful minerals paint the scene,
As microbes throw a festive spree.
With every scoop, a story told,
Of ancient feasts and treasures bold.

The dirt conceals a vibrant show,
Where minuscule artists come and go.
Each grain a brush, each root a pen,
Creating art again and again.

Sprouts peek out, as if to say,
"Look at us dance; we're on our way!"
With worms as muses, they all connect,
In this earthy realm, no one's a wreck.

So next time you dig, don't just see,
Look for the fun in that muddy spree.
For underneath our feet, with cheer,
Lies a gallery, waiting right here!

Ancient Echoes of the Earth

Listen close to the whispers low,
As rocks and roots put on a show.
The echoes from ancient times ring clear,
With giggles and nonsense—oh, what a cheer!

Old leaves crackle, telling tales,
Of dancing squirrels and tiny snails.
Each creak of branches is laughter bright,
As the earth holds parties through day and night.

Beneath our feet, a history thrives,
Where every root and fungus jives.
With mushrooms popping like confetti,
The underground is quite the spaghetti!

So next we walk this hallowed ground,
Remember the joy that can be found.
For in the earth's embrace, we know,
There's humor hidden in every row.

The Tapestry of Tilling

In the garden, worms gather round,
Doing the twist, shaking the ground.
Dancing with radishes, what a sight,
Even the carrots join in the light.

A farmer in boots, with a big grin,
Tripping on spades, that's how we win!
Rows of tomatoes are rumbling with glee,
'Let's grow a circus!' they yell with spree.

With weeds that laugh, in mischievous cheer,
Pretending to be dancers, oh dear!
A turnip's joke has the cucumbers roll,
While peas chuckle loud, losing control.

But when the rain falls, it's a slippery game,
Mud pies and glories, who's really to blame?
In this parade of green, we can all thrive,
In a messy ballet, we feel so alive.

Ballads of the Buried

Down in the dirt, a potato sings,
'Oh, what a daily joy that digging brings!'
Radical radishes on an underground spree,
Playing hide and seek, as happy as can be.

Carrots in capes, oh what a sight!
Vowing to grow tall, reaching for light.
They whisper their secrets, to the beet so wise,
'Let's start a band, to entertain the flies!'

Bees buzzing tunes, while the bugs tap their feet,
Each rhythm a story, sweet and neat.
Together they cheer, 'We'll rock this plot!'
As the sun sets down, dancing on the hot.

And when it's harvest time, the cheerleaders come,
With baskets and laughter, oh what a hum!
In this fun little world, where plants take the lead,
Every buried ballad will sprout like a seed.

Mother Earth's Anthem

Beneath blue skies, where gophers roam,
A chorus of veggies makes us feel at home.
Tomatoes in tutus, doing a jig,
While pumpkins roll by, doing their big dig.

Grains of laughter sprout, tall as can be,
Corn cobs with jokes, 'Hey, look at me!'
Kale's quirky tales leave everyone grinning,
As zucchinis do cartwheels, the day's just beginning.

"We're the green brigade!" they chant with delight,
"From dawn 'til dusk, we'll party tonight!"
The garlic throws garlic bread jokes, oh so bold,
As peppers plot pranks on the folks who are old.

But the funniest sight is the beans as they climb,
Racing for sun, in a race against time.
And Mother Earth chuckles, with infectious cheer,
For in this great garden, it's laughter we hear.

Cadence of the Crops

In the patch where the pumpkins wear silly hats,
The rhythm of radishes tap-dance with bats.
Underneath leafy canopies, laughter rings clear,
As the broccoli's banter draws everyone near.

The beets are the drummers, the weeds are the cheer,
"We'll grow a wise crop, so give us a year!"
With corn on the cob, crooning sweet tunes,
And peas in their pods, forming rock-band communes.

Each sprout has a story, their roots intertwine,
Sharing their secrets, oh how they shine!
Like rascally children playing outside,
In this dance of the harvest, we'll take it in stride.

So join in the chorus, where laughter is sown,
For every green giggle makes the garden grow.
With sunlight and joy, let's plant all we crave,
In this comical patch, we're forever brave!

The Melody of the Mossy Carpet

In the forest, where moss dreams,
Silly critters dance in teams.
Frogs croak tunes, and mushrooms sway,
Snails hold concerts every day.

Bouncing berries, red and round,
Bumblebees buzz, a joyful sound.
The ants march in their tiny bands,
With leaf trumpets in their hands.

Underneath the leafy shade,
Squirrels play a grand charade.
Rotting logs start to hum along,
The earth is where we all belong.

From muddy puddles, laughter swells,
As nature weaves its playful spells.
In the soil, fun is sown,
Under roots, where joy is grown.

Fables of the Fertile Earth

Worms tell tales of forgotten kings,
As pebbles gossip about shiny rings.
The daisies giggle at passing feet,
While dandelions offer up crazy treats.

Grasshoppers plan their moonlit show,
As beetles take the front-row glow.
A clever squirrel juggles acorns high,
While ants drop crumbs like confetti pie.

Mice write stories in the sand,
And turtles plot a marching band.
Nature laughs with every breeze,
Fables shared beneath the trees.

In this land where wild things roam,
Every crack is a cozy home.
With each sprout, a new tale begins,
In secrets whispered, nature grins.

Whispers of the Earth

If you listen, dirt will speak,
Of squishy joys and secrets unique.
The seeds giggle in their cozy beds,
While mushrooms bounce on leafy heads.

Wiggly worms in their mud disguise,
Play peek-a-boo with blinking eyes.
Bees tell tales of sweet delight,
As flowers twirl in colorful flight.

Rocks strategize their next big play,
As ants plot what to take away.
The wind sings softly, tickling leaves,
Where even the acorns dance in eaves.

Listen close, you might just hear,
The laughter of the earth, oh dear!
Every rustle, every cheer,
Is a reminder that joy is near.

Beneath the Surface

What happens where roots intertwine?
Dig deep down, you'll find it fine!
Chubby gophers throw their feast,
While moles concoct the cutest beast.

Underneath, it's a grand old ball,
With little creatures that stand tall.
The plants tell jokes, the fungi cheer,
Each party louder than the last year!

Mud pies are served with extra flair,
While tiny ants twirl without a care.
The laughter bubbles from every nook,
Beneath the grass, life's an open book.

So take a peek beneath your feet,
Where laughter and humble beings meet.
In this little world, bright and spry,
The fun of life will never die!

Resonance in the Ruins

In the cracks where daisies play,
Earthworms wiggle night and day.
The ants hold meetings, quite a scene,
Discussing plans to build their queen.

A tumbleweed laughs, rolls on by,
Singing tunes to the sky.
While rocks debate who's oldest here,
Even stones crack jokes with cheer.

Peeking mushrooms quirk a grin,
While moles plan a dance, their win.
A snobby root claims its height,
But tripped on vines—a silly sight!

The grass is green, but not too bright,
Telling tales of a nightlight bite.
And over there, a flower sighs,
With pollen dreams and buzzing flies.

Tones of Terrestrial Treasures

The potatoes gather for a show,
Winking at carrots down below.
Tomatoes throw shade with a laugh,
While pumpkins plot a chubby path.

A turnip wears a dapper hat,
And beans will dance like a jazzed up cat.
Beets are blushing, feeling bold,
As they trade stories about old gold.

Radishes roll, they can't resist,
While teasing peas, they can't coexist.
Onions cry, but it's all in jest,
They're playing hide and seek, they jest!

A garden gnome keeps the beat,
With a spade as his tapping feet.
Now lettuce tiptoes, oh so sly,
Ballet with sprouts, reaching for the sky.

Lamentations of the Loam

In shadows deep, the claybirds croon,
Poking fun at the sun and moon.
Gravel grumbles, 'I'm not that tough,'
While pebbles laugh, 'Too much is rough!'

A patch of thorns sings a ballad,
Of prickly love, oh what a salad!
Composting dreams, and giggles roar,
While weeds conspire, 'We want more!'

The crickets chirp, a tiny band,
With rhythmic feet, they make a stand.
As frogs decide to harmonize,
Chorus of croaks, 'We're quite the prize!'

A shifty snail joins in the mix,
Slime trails left, with clever tricks.
But earthworms roll their eyes in cheer,
Saying, 'Oh dear, here we go, dear!'

Songs Weaving Through the Roots

The roots do gather, ready to jam,
Tickling the toes of an eager fam.
With quirky vines that twist and twine,
They hum a tune, just feeling fine.

A sagebrush whispers, 'What's the plan?'
As lizards dance in a melty span.
Crickets tap out a raucous beat,
While sleepy bulbs sway to the heat.

Mushrooms nod, all dressed in style,
Creating poetry with a shy smile.
'Let's sway the ferns!' they softly plead,
A canopy dance, oh, what a lead!

The spinach joins, feeling so spry,
Twirling round as the sparrows fly.
Under the moon, a waltz in the dark,
Soil with songs—a joyful spark!

Dreaming in the Dark

In the night's cloak, the earth does heave,
Worms plot mischief, in whispers they weave.
Crickets hold court, with a chirp and a wink,
While shadows dance with a drink and a clink.

The night owl hoots, as the raccoons scheme,
Planting wild tales that undermine the dream.
A potato rolls over, unfurling its sprout,
"Join us for mischief!" it calls with a shout.

The moon looks down, with a giggle or two,
As daisies gossip in dresses of dew.
The garden sings softly, all secrets in tow,
While hedgehogs discuss the latest in show.

As dreams take flight beneath starlit skies,
Even the turnips are caught in surprise.
With laughter afloat, under moon's silver arc,
They flourish together, forever in the dark.

The Garden's Hidden Score

Underfoot, a symphony, all roots in a bind,
Carrots are orchestras, too shy to unwind.
Radishes tap dance, all dressed in their red,
While cabbage conducts with a nod of its head.

The tomatoes are blushing, a juicy delight,
As they hum along to the worms every night.
With laughter and sunshine, they play on repeat,
A concert of veggies, a garden's heartbeat.

The peas sing in harmony, bright little notes,
Chanting their dreams from their cozy green coats.
The zucchini rolls rhythm, a rhythmic delight,
Creating a melody under the moonlight.

A flower with petals too big for its head,
Sings of old tales that the roses have said.
In this tangled garden, both funny and sweet,
A hidden score plays with each shuffling beat.

Chants of the Broken Ground

Cracks in the earth sing of tales gone askew,
A taco plant grumbles, "What happened to stew?"
With chipmunks debating on peanut-shaped plots,
And ants marching in line, all gathering thoughts.

The tulips are gossiping, spilling old beans,
Of beetles who boasted about wild adventures and scenes.
While moles murmur soft, their secrets confined,
In worlds underground where the sun's hard to find.

The rocks sit aloof, with a smug little smirk,
As daisies get tangled and shriek, "We won't lurk!"
All together they harmonize, wild and absurd,
Chanting the chronicles, the tales unheard.

In this quirky patch of the crumbling ground,
An orchestra thrives, sweet harmony found.
With laughter and echoes, the soil has its say,
In the oddest of ways, it continues to play.

Euphony of the Ecosystem

In the garden's embrace, where the laughter does bloom,
Bees craft a buzz with a hint of perfume.
Ants in a line, they march with a jig,
While frogs offer croaks that are quite the big gig.

A rabbit's quick hop lands right on a beet,
"Oops!" it declares with a twirl of its feet.
The sunflowers turn, following rays of delight,
With whispers of winds that carry them light.

The cilantro and basil, a duo so fine,
Dance on the breeze, sipping dew like wine.
Every sprout on the rise, a player in swoon,
As mother nature conducts, beneath the warm moon.

In this grand little stage of the leafy brigade,
Each creature and plant has a part that's displayed.
With laughter and joy, they all freely play,
A euphony thrives, come what may.

www.ingramcontent.com/pod-product-compliance
Lightning Source LLC
Chambersburg PA
CBHW070314120526
44590CB00017B/2676